ELECTRICITY

SCIENCE SECRETS

Jason Cooper

The Rourke Corporation, Inc.
Vero Beach, Florida 32964

© 1992 The Rourke Corporation, Inc.

Edited by Sandra A. Robinson

PHOTO CREDITS

© Lynn M. Stone: title page, pages 4, 10, 12, 13, 17, 18;
© Joseph Antos: cover, page 7;
© Jerry Hennen: pages 8, 15, 21

LIBRARY OF CONGRESS
Library of Congress Cataloging-in-Publication Data
Cooper, Jason, 1942-
    Electricity / by Jason Cooper.
    p. cm. — (Science secrets)
    Includes index.
    Summary: Provides a simple discussion of natural and man-made
electricity and of how electrical power is generated and used.
    ISBN 0-86593-169-0
    1. Electricity—Juvenile literature. [1. Electricity.]
I. Series: Cooper, Jason, 1942-   Science secrets.
QC527.2.C67   1992
537—dc20   92-8812
                                              CIP
                                              AC

TABLE OF CONTENTS

Electricity   5
Electricity in Nature   6
Making Electricity   9
Sending Electricity   11
The Power of Electricity   14
Using Electricity   16
Carry-Out Electricity   19
Electricity and Safety   20
Pioneers in Electricity   22
Glossary   23
Index   24

ELECTRICITY

Electricity is one type of **energy,** or power. We think of electrical power as being in wires. But electricity, in one form or another, is all around us. For example, our bodies and other living things have electricity in them.

By controlling the electricity around us, by making it work for us, we have changed the world.

Controlled electricity: a light bulb

ELECTRICITY IN NATURE

The objects in our world are made up of invisible bits, or **particles.** One kind of particle is the **electron.** The power created by moving electrons—millions upon millions of them—is called electricity.

The activity of electrons in thunderclouds can form electric **currents** and huge sparks—flashes of lightning.

Lightning: electric currents in the sky

MAKING ELECTRICITY

People make electricity at electric power stations. Machines called **generators** make electricity from other forms of energy such as coal, falling water, wind, gas, oil or atomic energy.

The generator forces electrons into wires as a flow, or current, of electricity. Wires are known as **conductors** because they carry, or conduct, the electrical current.

Atomic-powered electric plant

SENDING ELECTRICITY

Electric current travels through conductors to homes, factories and other places.

Electricity enters your home in wires made of metal, usually copper or aluminum. Metal is a good conductor.

Electric current is much like water that rushes through a hose. When you close the hose nozzle, the flow, or current, stops. You control the flow of electricity with on-off switches.

Towers lift electric power lines

Radar screen powered by electricity

Electric-powered "sky cars"

THE POWER OF ELECTRICITY

A streak of lightning, wild as the wind, bolts across the sky. It may strike the ground, or it may not. It is like an angry, uncaged rattlesnake. Its uncontrolled electrical power is enormous. And even a broken electric power line can change soil into glass!

The electricity made in power stations is controlled for our use. It is forced into wires. But like lightning, it produces heat, power and light.

Broken line changing soil into glass

USING ELECTRICITY

We use the energy of electricity in our homes, schools, businesses, hospitals and science laboratories. Electricity warms our food, lights our buildings, and powers many of our machines.

Electricity has helped bring the countries of the world closer by speeding up and improving communication. Our telephones, televisions, and other communications instruments all run on electricity.

A diesel electric train

PHOTO special

RAY VAC
Heavy Duty
MAXIMUM

SIZE D
BATTERY

MN1300 1.5 VOLTS

CAUTION: DO NOT CONNECT IMPROPERLY.
CHARGE OR DISPOSE OF IN FIRE. BATTERY MAY
EXPLODE OR LEAK.
Made in U.S.A.

DURACELL

ALKALINE BATTERY

DURACELL
ALKALINE BATTERY

DURACELL

MN1500   1.5 VOLTS
CAUTION: DO NOT CONNECT IMPROPERLY.
CHARGE OR DISPOSE OF IN FIRE. BATTERY
MAY EXPLODE OR LEAK.   MADE IN U.S.A.

SIZE AA
BATTERY

PX ALKALINE   Leakproof Guarantee

CARRY-OUT ELECTRICITY

Wires conduct electricity from power stations to homes and factories. But how do people get electricity when they are not at home or work? They use "carry-out" electricity—a **battery.**

Batteries are containers filled with chemicals and metal. The action that takes place between the metal and chemicals makes electricity.

Batteries help power cameras, trains, radios, toys and many other things.

Batteries: carry-out electricity

ELECTRICITY AND SAFETY

Electricity can be a powerful friend—or enemy. An electric shock, or jolt of electricity, can hurt or even kill someone.

"High Voltage" signs mean strong electric currents are nearby. Stay away.

Avoid lightning, too. Stay in a building or in a hard-topped vehicle during thunderstorms. Also—if your hands or feet are wet, do not touch electric devices.

Workmen repair damaged electric line

PIONEERS IN ELECTRICITY

Scientists began many experiments with electricity in the 1700s. In 1752, Benjamin Franklin used a kite to prove that lightning was electricity.

But people did not begin to control and use electricity until about 100 years ago. Thomas Edison, an inventor, began a small electric company in New York City in 1882. Edison offered electric lights to 400 customers.

Glossary

battery (BAH ter ee) — a mixture of metal and chemicals that make electricity in a package of some kind

conductor (kuhn DUK ter) — that which can carry, or conduct, something, such as a copper wire that conducts electricity

current (KER ent) — the flow, or ongoing passage of something, such as the flow of electrons

electron (e LEK trahn) — one of the invisible bits, or particles, in the natural make-up of all things

energy (EN er gee) — power; the ability to do work

generator (JEHN er a ter) — a machine that makes, or produces, electric power

particles (PAR tuh kullz) — tiny, sometimes invisible bits of matter, such as electrons

INDEX

batteries   19

chemicals   19

communications   16

conductors   9, 11

Edison, Thomas   22

electric shock   20

electricity

   control of   5, 11, 14, 22

   currents of   6, 9, 11

   power of   5, 14

   safety with   20

   uses of   16, 19

electrons   6

energy   5, 9

Franklin, Benjamin   22

generator   9

heat   14

light   14

lightning   6, 14, 20, 22

lights, electric   16, 22

power line   14

power stations   9, 14, 19

thunderclouds   6

thunderstorms   20

wires   5, 9, 11, 14